Paperback ISBN: 978-1-955411-17-2

E-book ISBN: 978-1-955411-22-6

Hardcover ISBN: 978-1-955411-20-2

Library of Congress Control Number: 2023924327

Printed by Davis and Greer Publishing
in the United States of America

To the reader

The struggle and pain you feel are only temporary. Remember, in order to heal, you sometimes have to poke the wound. By remembering how it came about, you'll finally be able to bandage the wound, move on, and heal.

Hope
after the
storm

Chrishana Greer

Contents

CHAPTER 1

I remember...

I remember...

when my uncle took my innocence at such an early age. It probably was when I was in the third or fourth grade.

I remember...

the first time he came into my room.

I remember...

everywhere I went within my own home,
he was there.

Basement, living room, bedroom
—ready to repeat the cycle.
The first time he came into my room.

I remember...

my mother constantly being at work,
and she was always tired.
So, who was I to tell?

I remember...

*those days when it would happen in the
back room of my grandmother's basement
apartment as she laid in the living room on
the couch, balled under a blanket,
with no clue what was going on
within her home.*

I remember...

when he started coming around less.
I got older, and it eventually stopped.

I remember...

going through life without saying a
word about what happened,
until one day, I suddenly forgot.

I remember...

that college wasn't an option.
School just wasn't for me.

I remember...

entering the military to escape
the broken foundation I came from.

I remember...

when it happened again, and this time,
I was even more confused.

I remember...

that confusion turning into depression. Yet, I still laced up my green combat boots every day.

I remember...

*seeking a clearer understanding of
what had happened to me from a
strong Black woman who had served
and gone through life longer than I had.*

I remember...

*still not understanding, because I hadn't
been beaten or damaged physically,
which was my understanding of abuse.
So, what had really happened to me?*

I remember...

*describing the details to military
authorities and the victim advocate.
Still trying to wrap my head around
how this could be true.
I was even more confused.*

I remember...

long, scary nights when I couldn't sleep. Instead, I would sit up, waiting for that knock on the door from the higher-ranking airman who had done this to me.

I remember...

those days without eating.
I had no appetite, and a single
piece of candy could last me for days.

I remember...

when my lack of appetite turned into a deeper depression. Yet, I still smiled, even though military life had been beating my ass for a while.

I remember...

putting on my airman battle uniform
and lacing my boots to go to a place
where no one is allowed to show any hurt.

I remember...

*when I started looking over my shoulder
because I knew he might be watching.*

I remember...

my heart pounding and racing from being in large, crowded spaces. Not knowing if he was near and just blending in.

I remember...

finally telling my mother, without
revealing the details of what had taken place.
Until she replied that it was assault.

Instantly thinking, 'Dang, assault?
How could that be when I wasn't beaten?'

The thought triggered memories of how
her brother had handled me.

I remember...

my mother being surprised that an assault had happened when I was young, and from her brother, but she showed no sense of concern.

I remember...

*the news of what had happened to me
as an adult spreading through the family,
as if they were happy I had gone through it.*

I remember...

my father's family attacking me because of what I had gone through, as if they'd prayed for this moment.

I remember...

the rumors about me dating a captain and crying rape.

I remember...

a relative, writing me,
"That's why you got raped."
As if she was happy it
had happened to me.

I remember...

being mad, because I wondered how my parents could break my trust.

I remember...

feeling alone while wearing a smile,
even though most of me was
already dead inside.

I remember...

being attacked on social media by women and men, some who wore the same military uniform as me, defending and protecting a coward.

I remember...

the court martial, where airmen-those
I had looked at as friends-took the stand
and tried to discredit my character.

I remember...

him going to prison and losing it all.

I remember...

going to therapy but not being able to speak.

I remember...

getting out of the military,
going back home, and getting pregnant.
I thought my life would go back to normal,
but it was never the same.

I remember...

my father's family telling my daughter's dad that our child wasn't his. Instead, it was the baby of the Navy officer I had dated and cried rape on.

I remember...

moving out of state to escape Chicago,
where I knew I didn't belong.
Running to a place where I wasn't known.
Where I wouldn't be judged,
attacked, and belittled.

I remember...

therapists came and left. They just couldn't seem to get me to connect.

I remember...

after he got out of prison, the master sergeant who had caused my military sexual trauma was following me on Goodreads. Initially, I thought it was a coincidence; after all, his was a common name. Then it went from Goodreads to social media.

I remember...

him speaking of my daughter,
as if he knew everything about me.

I remember...

him telling ME he has PTSD
from what I did to him.

I remember...

*him going to court and standing in front
of a judge, who handed him back
everything he had lost.*

I remember...

that same day, trying to kill myself.

I remember...

being tired of trying to be strong
for people who didn't give a damn
how life had beaten me.

I remember...

finally getting a therapist who could get me to tell the story of what had happened to me. But she couldn't get me to release the emotional connection.

I remember...

women's group after women's group for women who had gone through military sexual trauma, just like me. Week after week, we would meet, and I would listen to different military and personal life stories. I still couldn't form any words.

I remember...

*finally finding a group that made me
want to dig deep into my emotions
to process what had happened to me.*

CHAPTER 2

I felt...

I felt...

emotions I couldn't process. How was I? I was still living it. The only thing the military had done was place us in two different buildings, until I got orders to transfer to another base. Even then, I still couldn't escape the rape.

I felt...

that maybe on another base back in the States, there would be no more whispers. That maybe I'd get to be a typical airman and have a chance at my career. Nope—even then, I couldn't escape it. The other airmen didn't know what had happened to me, but I still had to deal with my attorney overseas. The constant reminder led me back to therapy, where I couldn't talk, even though I wanted to. I was afraid that anything said in therapy would be misinterpreted and used against me. There I was, back in the States, yet my issues followed me wherever I went.

I felt...

tired. Eventually, I was sick of it all,
and I didn't want the military career anymore.
I just wanted to be a typical
twenty-one-year-old and go back home.

I felt...

*defeated and used, like a rag that had been
dragged through the mud, with no one
there to say, "Hey, let's help clean her up."
When that was really all I needed.*

I felt...

like I finally knew what it meant to be just a number; just a body. See, the military conditions you to believe that they have your back and we're a family. Until it's time to use those core values that the good ol' Air Force shouts and raves about. Maybe those core values apply only to the airmen with lighter skin and straighter hair.

I felt...

that ultimately, the military had failed me . . .
betrayed me. My squadron, commander, peers,
and leadership had let me down,
leaving me to figure out and go through
this traumatizing stage alone.

I felt...

attacked by the military and members of my squadron during the court martial and online.

I felt...

traumatized. I had already faced the horrific trauma of the assault. Now, I had to deal with the repercussions of reporting.
The trauma of no one believing my story because it didn't align with their experiences or beliefs on sexual assault.
The whispers, the stares, the walk of shame—as if I'd done something wrong.

I felt...

the constant attacks from everyone. My family, the military, social media. I couldn't escape it. For my family, it was just something to just talk about. To my military peers, I was public enemy number one because I was an airman and he was a master sergeant.

I felt...

emptiness. As if no matter where I had gone in life, I wasn't meant to have a solid foundation. I wasn't meant to have genuine people around me who actually cared for me and wanted me to succeed and do better in life. Instead, I was meant to simply survive. I would never be one of those people who got to experience actual love from a family or friends. No matter where I went or how I tried to get that experience, even an ounce of it, it just wasn't meant for me.

CHAPTER 3

I overcame...

I overcame...

life. At least I thought I did.

I overcame...

the adversaries. Eventually I fought back. I spoke up. I removed and deleted anyone from my life who had thought my story of pain and assault was a joke. I removed those people who looked at my circumstances as a "happy it was her" situation.

I overcame...

by accepting that there were so many different odds against me. Instead of being mad, I decided to do everything I was never supposed to do. I attended and graduated college, remained a great mother, released a few children's books with my daughter, traveled the world, and became a very successful businesswoman. Yeah, my trust and outlook on people were still fucked up. But what would you expect from someone who had gone through what I did in life? I had to push forward through it all.

I overcame...

the feelings of hurt, embarrassment, shame, and guilt based on other people's views of me and the labels attached to me by people who knew nothing about me. I knew exactly who I was. I knew I could no longer allow everyone else's opinions of me to dictate how I saw myself or felt toward myself. I was no longer the little girl in third or fourth grade, and I damn sure wasn't the twenty-year-old kid in the military. Although I went through everything that I had gone through, it didn't define me. The reality was, I had made it further than my family and people I once considered friends had wanted me to. I made it further than the military had expected me to. And I was okay with that.

I overcame...

*the humiliation and discomfiture that came
with being raped as a kid and again as an
adult. It was an awful stage in my life that
would forever be attached to me. But, I was
going to be okay. I hadn't done any of those
things to myself. These were the actions
of others. Yes, I went through it. But these
were the actions of my uncle and the actions
of someone superior in the military. Their
actions were not my actions. It wasn't me.
Accepting that I didn't cause this to happen
to me was how I overcame everything.
I finally understood that it was time
for me to heal.*

CHAPTER 4

I started healing...

I started healing...

and I am still on that road. I would be lying if I said I was completely healed, because I am a long way from it. But I am on my way.

I started healing...

by watching who I allow around me and in my personal space. I Understand that not everyone has my best interests at heart, and that's fine. As long as I am doing what I believe is best for me, that is what matters.

I started healing...

*by stepping outside my comfort zone.
Trying to get out and engage more while still
understanding how far I can go without being
triggered and taken into a dark space that no
one will be able to get me out of but myself.*

I started healing...

by not being concerned by people's negative thoughts toward me. Most of these people hadn't accomplished nearly half of what I had.

I started healing...

by joining Pilates to help me build social skills that come with being in public.

I started healing...

by realizing I am not the only person who has gone through something like this in their life.

I started healing...

by utilizing the resources available to me as a Veteran so I can meet people who have gone through some of the same stuff I have where I don't feel the pressure of meeting someone new whose story is completely different from mine or worry that they are trying to gain information about me with an ulterior motive.

I started healing...

by writing my thoughts down. Once I was able to write and process what had happened to me in my life from my sexual trauma, from childhood to the service, it started to give me clarity, and I realized I needed help processing some of those emotions.

I started healing...

by realizing that it was completely normal to get professional help and speak about what I had gone through in a judgment-free zone where whatever was discussed between those four walls stayed within those four walls.

I started healing...

by distancing myself from those who weren't good for my mental health. Those people who brought more negative energy with their presence.

I started healing...

by recognizing that I would never be the same person I was before those horrific things happened to me. But I was going to become better, day by day, as I did what I needed to complete to heal within myself.

I started healing...

by recognizing that people are who they are. They talk, they gossip, and they spread stories. People are people. Their actions don't determine who I am.

I started healing...

once I no longer wanted my
trauma to dictate my life.

I started healing...

after I accepted that there was absolutely NOTHING normal about me anymore. I'll never be a normal person. I'll never live a normal life, or even think as I did before the military sexual assault and aftermath. But I would be as normal as I could be. If what I went through made me normally DIFFERENT, I acknowledged that. I began viewing life from the lens of a thirty-year-old woman who had gone through things in life. I accepted that I couldn't go back and change the stories in my life that had already happened.

I started healing...

when will you?

End Message to the Reader

I wrote this book with the hopes of allowing the reader to understand that we all go through adversity in life. However, those things will never be able to define you if you don't let it. It's perfectly acceptable to tell your story without telling your story, whether it be detail to detail or a short lay out like the one above. But, as long as you understand that you're the narrator that's when you gain your control back. Everything is going to be okay. I faced some of my darkest days alone. And those dark times do not control your destiny or mine.

www.ingramcontent.com/pod-product-compliance
Lightning Source LLC
Chambersburg PA
CBHW040847120626
46547CB00001B/64